SHAPES, SHAPES EVERYWHERE

Albatros

The world around us is full of shapes. Why do we see them everywhere? What shapes do we recognize? And what do they tell us?

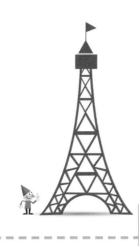

WHAT ARE SHAPES

and how are they important to us?

Take a look around. Much of what you see is made up of shapes you've been familiar with your whole life: rectangles, squares, circles, and triangles. We find them everywhere and in all kinds of forms. Shapes have many properties that make them very effective, and lots of things wouldn't work without them.

First of all, let's brush up on a few shapes:

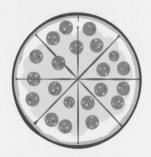

This traffic sign is in the shape of a triangle.

This pizza is in the shape of a circle.

This textbook is in the shape of a rectangle.

This chessboard is in the shape of a square (and is also divided into squares).

When we talk about **shapes**, we mean simple objects on a flat plane—that is to say, flat objects that have two dimensions (length and width) and that can be drawn on a sheet of paper.

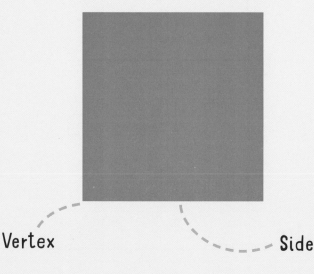

Vertex

Side

Shapes usually have **sides**, and the number of sides helps us tell the difference between individual shapes. The place where the sides meet is called the **vertex**.

The science of shapes is called **geometry**.

To explain what makes some shapes special, let's look at two important properties of the sides of geometric shapes: being **parallel** and being **perpendicular**.

Perpendicular lines meet at a right angle. For example, the sides of a wardrobe are perpendicular to the floor, pointing up toward the ceiling. Similarly, trees grow perpendicular to the ground, pointing up toward the sun.

Parallel lines—like parallel roads you drive down—are lines that do not cross over each other. They are like roads without an intersection. Even if we could stretch them to infinity, they would always be straight and would never meet or cross each other.

Can you find the parallel and perpendicular lines in this room?

- -

And now it's time to look at basic shapes and their properties . . .

A **square** has four sides of the same length. The opposite sides are parallel. The adjacent sides are perpendicular. And that's not all—when we connect the opposite vertices, we create diagonals, and they too are perpendicular to each other!

A **triangle** has three sides and therefore three vertices. The sides can be different lengths, and two of them can be perpendicular.

A **circle** has only one side. It also has an infinite number of vertices, since every point on a circle is a vertex. Fascinating, isn't it?

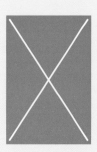

A **rectangle** differs from a square in that it has two opposite pairs of sides that are the same length, but one pair is a different length than the other. They are also parallel and perpendicular to each other, but the diagonals of the rectangle are not perpendicular.

OK, enough geometry! Let's go take a look at the world of shapes!

We've created a rectangular protest sign. We are protesting against pineapple on pizza!

Shapes that make it easier
TO COMMUNICATE

People might speak a ton of different languages, but shapes help us understand what we want to say more easily. Thanks to the rectangular stamp and the round postmark, the postcard that we're impatiently awaiting will arrive. And thanks to the message on the fridge, we're able to read what we have to buy.

Every flag with shapes represents one letter. *Ahoy!*

The rectangular traffic sign says that we can't go more than 20 miles per hour as we approach the school.

Emojis in cell phone messages and tablets help us show our emotions. When we see these yellow circles, we can imagine our friends' faces.

WHAT'S UP? 😊

☹ BAD DAY . . .

Tom can't find the emergency exit! Luckily he noticed this rectangular sign!

JANE MCGILL
322 OAK ST.
ARLINGTON, TX 76017

Just stick a rectangular stamp on the letter to Grandma and it will get there safely.

Shapes that create
ORDER

Shapes allow us to look at schedules, read instructions or directions, and even pay the right price in a store. Some shapes announce rules needed to avoid chaos around us. They can be flexible (for example, you can switch off your alarm clock to get more sleep), but there are also some very strict shapes. Traffic signs are a good example, and it makes sense to obey them at all times.

What do we have now, Victor? Math or PE? Why don't you take a look at the schedule on the board?

If drivers spot white rectangles on the road, they should stop and allow people to cross the road safely. Shall we help you cross to the other side?

We can go now! That round green light on the traffic light is on!

According to the rectangular train station sign, we still have time ... Our train leaves in a quarter of an hour. And then home at last!

10:19

A circular clock face is merciless! Get up and go to school, it's already morning!

John wants to know how much cough syrup to take. But how is he ever going to find out from these long rectangular instructions?

When Anna pays with a rectangular dollar bill, she receives change in the form of some round coins.

George cuts the lemon into perfect round slices to make lemonade. Watch out for those fingers!

The burners on the stove are as round as the bottoms of pans. I wonder what's for dinner today?

Shapes
AT HOME

We see them all around our homes. Slices of bread, cheese, or cucumber have their own specific shapes. Plates and dishes are usually round. And what about the bathroom? The rectangular mirror above the sink helps us make ourselves look like we're walking out of a fashion magazine every day.

No one makes blankets from crocheted squares quite like my Grandma Matilda!

Mom's prepared triangular sandwiches for the kids to take to school. Don't take them all, Tommy!

Today, Mike is shaving for the first time and looking in the rectangular mirror to make sure he doesn't miss even the tiniest whisker.

My cousins use so many makeup tools to do their makeup! Round powder boxes and puffs, rectangular eye shadow—it's way too complicated for me!

Shapes as SYMBOLS

Some shapes remind us so much of a particular meaning that they have become symbols used in all cultures. So we can use the shapes instead of words. Think about a rectangular flag. If you look at the flags people wave at sports stadiums or Fourth of July parades, you know what they support. But shapes can also symbolize important values in life. The rings that the bride and groom exchange at weddings tell us about their devotion to each other.

The bride and groom are exchanging rings as a sign of their loyalty. Who's got the rings?

As you can see in the pie chart, 20% of viewers watched the last episode, and according to the bar chart, the popularity of the series keeps increasing.

The triangles on these doors suggest a laboratory experiment might be going on inside.

Fans from all over the world come together at this international sporting event, waving national flags to support their country's athletes. Go team!

Arrows in the shape of a triangle are the symbol for recycling. The waste in this bin will be recycled and used to make new products.

Jacob is drawing the symbol of peace in his notebook. He may or may not know that the circle with four lines was originally the sign used by the campaign against nuclear weapons.

OTHER FLAT SHAPES

Back to geometry

Squares, rectangles, triangles, and circles—that's not all there is. Other shapes can be formed by combining these basic shapes or by changing them.

What other flat shapes do you know?

A **trapezium** is quadrilateral, which means it has four sides. One pair of its opposite sides are parallel, but of different lengths.

A **star**, in this case a five-pointed star, is also a polygon.

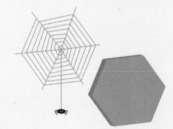

A **hexagon** has six sides. If all the sides are the same length, they form a regular hexagon, which we can see in the shapes of honeycombs and cobwebs.

All sides of a **rhombus** are the same length. Its opposite sides are parallel and its diagonals are perpendicular to each other. But unlike with a square, its diagonals are of different lengths. Also, the adjacent sides are not perpendicular to each other.

An **oval**, like a circle, has no sides or angles and its outline is formed by an infinite number of vertices. So how is it different from a circle? The vertices of a circle are all exactly the same distance from its center, which is not the case with an oval. An oval is shaped more like an egg.

Axisymmetry

Certain geometric shapes are **symmetrical** along one or more **axes**. What does this mean? Well, imagine a shape cut out of paper. When you fold it down the middle—that is to say, along its axis—it divides into two exact halves that match each other at all points.

Some shapes, such as isosceles **triangles**, have only one axis of symmetry.

Other shapes, such as **rectangles** or rhombuses, have two axes of symmetry.

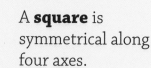

A **square** is symmetrical along four axes.

A **circle**—which just always has to be special now, doesn't it?!—has an infinite number of axes of symmetry.

We also find symmetry in everyday life.

We can also talk about shapes without talking about geometry. A detective can catch a criminal by the pattern on his shoe, and a locksmith can copy the shape of a key and create duplicate keys for a whole family. In short, the world really is full of shapes. So where else can we find them?

On the following pages, you'll find examples of everything we have just learned about . . .

Shapes that help us find our WAY AROUND

Because they are clearly recognizable, even from a distance, shapes act as invaluable aids when we are trying to find our way or get a quick sense of where we are. With traffic signs, the shape has a meaning. Do you know which sign shape means "caution" and which means "prohibited"?

Let's follow the arrows. The signpost says we're going the right way.

VISITOR CENTER 0.2 miles

MUSEUM 0.3 MILES

RESTROOM 50 feet

STATUE 0.1 miles

PARK 0.5 miles

It's a good thing Granddad brought his old compass. We'd be lost without this circular invention.

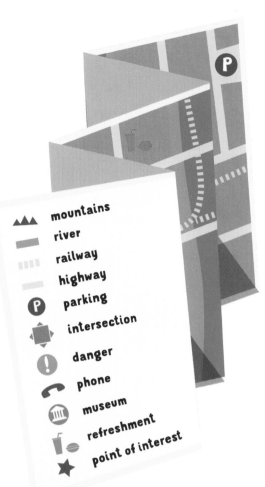

Every map needs a legend. This tells us the meaning of the individual shapes so we know how to find our way on the map.

mountains
river
railway
highway
P **parking**
intersection
! **danger**
phone
museum
refreshment
point of interest

Look, a sign for the emergency room! They'll surely be able to tell you whether you have the flu or pneumonia.

We can immediately recognize Italy on a map—it's famously shaped like a boot!

Rob is always confused. Are restrictive traffic signs in the shape of a triangle or an octagon?

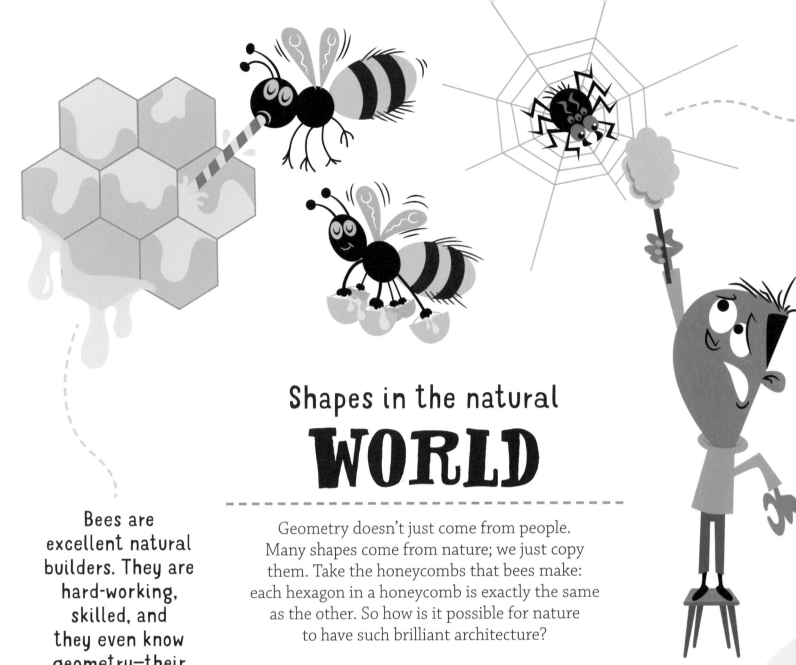

Shapes in the natural
WORLD

Geometry doesn't just come from people. Many shapes come from nature; we just copy them. Take the honeycombs that bees make: each hexagon in a honeycomb is exactly the same as the other. So how is it possible for nature to have such brilliant architecture?

Bees are excellent natural builders. They are hard-working, skilled, and they even know geometry—their honeycombs are made of hexagons.

Wow, look at that! The diver has found a beautiful starfish. It's amazing what nature can do.

A spider has built a regular octagonal web in our living room. Hey, get out of here!

Snowflakes are beautifully symmetrical. Each one is different, and you can have lots of fun with them!

The ladybug is unmistakable—a red shell and seven dots. You know it immediately.

Thomas is learning about different kinds of trees—you can tell them apart by the shapes of the leaves.

A bolt wouldn't work without a hexagonal nut.

Shapes that help
US OUT

Shapes have unique features that are very important for us. They can protect us or let us call for help. Certain shapes can even save lives. Round pills are easy to swallow and help us recover from illnesses. Outside the U.S., a warning triangle (rather than a traffic cone) is the international symbol of a breakdown or crash ahead. This can help prevent further accidents. And let's not forget the lifering!

My vacation isn't going too well—I've just had an accident! I've put the warning triangle on the road, though, so that other drivers know.

Don't worry, you'll feel better after you've taken this round pill.

If I don't find the shape of the key that fits in this keyhole, I'll never get into the house!

Brian has learned to fasten his buttons. Sometimes it's hard with these tiny circles, but it's better than being cold.

The crossing guard has stopped the cars with her sign so that the children can cross safely.

Here, catch the lifering! It's a good thing I was passing by, or else you might have drowned.

Shapes for
DECORATING

Polka dots, stripes, and knitted patterns—all are made of the basic shapes we see around us, and we love using them for decoration. Different cultures have their own traditional patterns of clothing or decoration that are known all around the world. Jewelry often comes in the shape of a ring or ball, because it fits perfectly on your finger or around your neck and doesn't scratch your skin.

The patterns of traditional Scottish kilts are a profusion of squares and rectangles. Beauty in simplicity!

At Christmas, all members of the Campbell family wear sweaters with cheerful, striking geometrical patterns. Everyone has to keep up the tradition.

The candles on the cake are lit and we've hung garlands full of triangles all around the room. Time to call in the birthday boy!

Grandma's box is full of valuable jewelry. Every ring or pair of earrings has its own story.

Joanna absolutely loves polka dots! She'd like to have them on all her clothes.

Photographs in various rectangular frames remind us of all those we love.

A little look at solid objects
3 DIMENSIONAL SHAPES

Until now, we have dealt mainly with flat shapes. But the shapes around us are not just two-dimensional. Oh no, shapes (like the other things around us) usually have not only length and width, but also depth. We can touch them, throw them around, stack them up on top of each other. We can glue them together or carve them out of wood.

For shapes in space, we distinguish between length, width, and height. These objects are three-dimensional—also known as 3D—because they exist in **three dimensions**. We also call these objects solids.

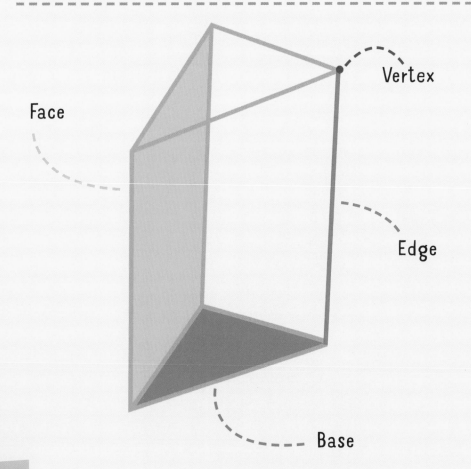

Face

Vertex

Edge

Base

Like flat shapes, solids have **vertices**, which means the points where three **edges** meet. Edges are the places where two **faces** meet. So what are faces? These are simply areas on the surface of a three-dimensional shape. In the case of our prism, they are in the shape of rectangles.

You may be thinking: What about the face at the bottom? The triangular one? Well, it's called the base and it is the **base** of our prism. It differs from the other faces in its shape.

Let's learn the names of some basic solids!

Cuboid

This is a kind of prism, which means it is a solid that has two bases facing each other, and these are connected by parallel edges. This prism has a rectangular base, so its faces are also rectangular. The two faces opposite each other are always the same. A book, for example, is cuboid in its shape.

Cone

A cone is like a pyramid with a circular base. If we slice a cone in half from top to bottom, the flat face of each half would be shaped like a triangle. This is the shape of traffic cones.

Cube

A cube is a special kind of cuboid whose edges are all the same length. Thus, all the faces of a cube are square. Playing dice are cubes.

Cylinder

The bases of the cylinder are mostly circular and are connected by parallels, so it is similar to a cuboid. If we were to cut a cylinder in half, the flat face would be rectangular in shape. A roll of toilet paper is cylindrical.

Pyramid

The base of a pyramid can have three or more straight sides and angles—shapes we call polygons. However, a pyramid differs from a prism in that it has only one base and the edges of the faces converge to one point—the apex. The faces of the pyramid are therefore triangular. The Great Pyramids in Egypt are named after this shape.

Sphere

A sphere is a solid object with no edges or vertices— only a surface. All points on the surface of a sphere are equally distant (or equidistant) from the common center. A ball is a sphere.

Now let's be done with all of this theorizing and go back to observing the world around us. See if you can find all of the three-dimensional shapes on the following pages.

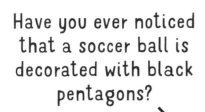

Have you ever noticed that a soccer ball is decorated with black pentagons?

My granddad loves playing cards. Hearts, spades, diamonds, or clubs—he always plays a good hand.

Shapes we
PLAY WITH

Without shapes, we couldn't enjoy ball and board games. Shapes are a big part of games and toys. The symbols on playing cards are important for the rules of Poker and Blackjack, and you couldn't play Ludo without dice. And just think of all the games played with balls of all sizes! In short, you can have a lot of fun with shapes and geometry.

I'm looking forward to flying my kite this fall. I'm certain mine will fly the highest!

It's a good thing we found the die. We wouldn't know how many squares to move without it.

If Paul takes one more prism out of the tower, it will fall down and Edith will be the winner!

You can only step once in each square, and it must be in the correct order . . . The rules of hopscotch are simple, but it's quite the workout!

Shapes in
MUSIC

Shapes are great to listen to, and they can record and reproduce our favorite songs. That's right, geometric shapes are a fundamental part of music. Music starts with a rectangular piece of sheet music, on which we write musical notes. We then play the composition on musical instruments of various shapes. After that, we can record the music onto a round CD or a round record. Finally we listen to it played through cuboid-shaped speakers.

Is that a triangular guitar? No, it's a balalaika!

Play the notes correctly, Brett! Don't you know that the shape of the note defines its length?

I can't imagine Mediterranean music without the tambourine. It's just a little round drum with littler round cymbals, but it really creates a big sound!

Julie will play the triangle in this song, because she can keep the rhythm.

Phillip collects vinyl records. They're not the latest technology, but the sound on this black circle is the best!

Each bar on a xylophone is different in size and therefore plays a different note than the others.

THE SHAPES

Oh no! My brother is practicing his drums again! He bought a full set of cylindrical drums and circular cymbals. What an ungodly racket he makes!

Proper cuboid-shaped speakers can fill any large space with sound. Just watch out for your ears!

Shapes in
SPORTS

Julie is weaving around the cones to learn how to skate. Look how fast she's going!

They slide, they spin, they even fly! Geometric shapes are super important to all sports. Take track and field events, for example—you run on an oval track, you jump into a rectangular landing pit, and you throw the shot put, the discus, and the javelin. What other shapes are in your favorite sports?

Breathe in, breathe out . . . Every yogi finds their inner calm on the rectangular mat.

Exercises on the balance beam are really tricky. It's so narrow that the slightest mistake can end in a fall from this narrow cuboid.

Catching a spinning frisbee isn't easy, but it's a breeze for Cooper, the neighbor's dog.

We have to practice the handover to have a chance of winning the relay race on the oval-shaped track.

That looks like a world record! What a throw! The discus in still in the air!

Nice strike, Luke! Your ball is going to knock all the bowling pins down.

Shapes that show our
ACCOMPLISHMENTS

Badges, awards, diplomas—these shapes show our accomplishments. We can show them off and proudly fasten them to our chests, or just be thankful that we have achieved them. They are a reward for participation, in sports or in education. Whatever the case, they help us feel proud.

It's not every day that you take part in swimming competitions. Natalie can now take home a rectangular diploma for competing.

Mark finally got his university diploma. He's received this rolled-up piece of paper after years of hard work!

Tom deserved the gold medal for his unsurpassable jump! He will display this round piece of metal at home, so that every guest can admire it.

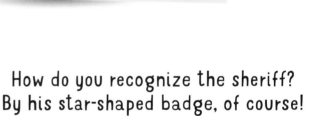

Ryan still hasn't got his "being quiet" badge. Could you manage not to say a single word all day?

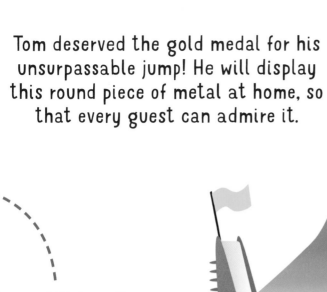

How do you recognize the sheriff? By his star-shaped badge, of course!

All the best, Sam! What a beautiful cylindrical cake! Time to blow out the candles!

Phew, I'm glad we got all our boxes into the elevator! I was afraid that it wouldn't fit into this small cuboid.

Shapes that get things
MOVING

A slide, a car wheel, a helicopter blade, or a flat paddle—have you ever noticed that all these shapes have one thing in common? They move things, machines, or people. The combination of their unique shape and the earth's gravity or the air makes many things easier to do . . . and fun to do!

Oh no, I have to paddle fast! There's a shark coming! There's that frighteningly familiar shape of its fin!

Good thing the castaway built a stable square-shaped raft. He wouldn't have made it off the island otherwise.

Oh no, there's a hole in the tire! Dad will have to replace it with the spare.

How do bicyclists ride uphill like it's no big deal? It's the gears on the bicycle—the smaller the cogwheel the chain uses, the easier it is to pedal.

Off we go! The slide forms a large triangle, which means it's good for sliding.

I really like abstract and cubist works. Even geometry can be art!

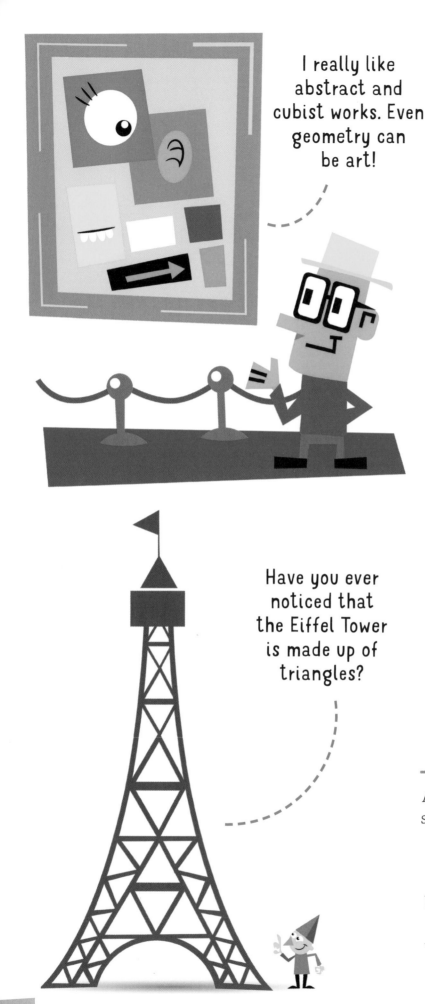

Have you ever noticed that the Eiffel Tower is made up of triangles?

Shapes
IN ART

Architecture and fine art involve observing the shapes around us and depicting and combining them. Without geometry, buildings wouldn't even be standing. And as we can see from Egyptian pyramids, shapes have been used in art since ancient times. But even modern technology in art, such as videos, would not have been possible without shapes. Shall we create a work of art based on the shapes we have learned?

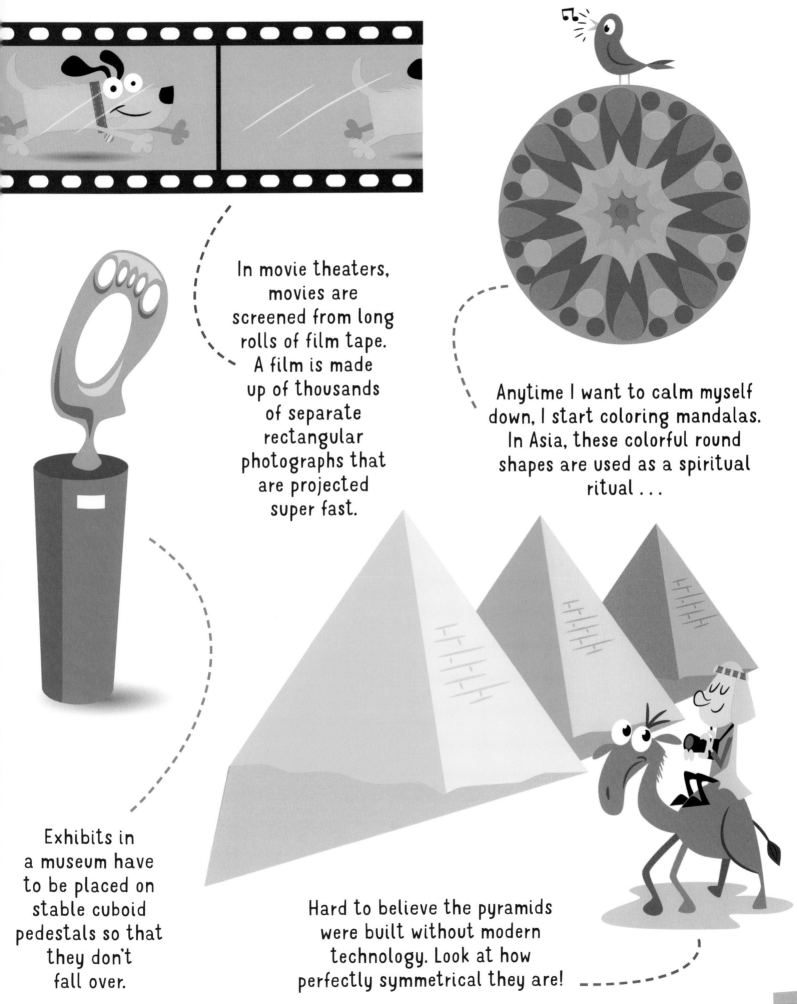

In movie theaters, movies are screened from long rolls of film tape. A film is made up of thousands of separate rectangular photographs that are projected super fast.

Anytime I want to calm myself down, I start coloring mandalas. In Asia, these colorful round shapes are used as a spiritual ritual . . .

Exhibits in a museum have to be placed on stable cuboid pedestals so that they don't fall over.

Hard to believe the pyramids were built without modern technology. Look at how perfectly symmetrical they are!

© B4U Publishing for Albatros,
an imprint of Albatros Media Group, 2023
5. května 1746/22, Prague 4, Czech Republic
Written by Lenka Chytilová
Illustrations © Gary Boller
Translated by Mark Worthington
Edited by Scott Alexander Jones

Printed in China by Leo Paper Group